A Tale of Two Cities

a musical play based on the novel by
Charles Dickens

Book by Dave Ross and Vivienne Carter

Music and lyrics by Dave Ross, Neil Parker
and Michael Mullane

SAMUELFRENCH.COM
SAMUELFRENCH-LONDON.CO.UK

A TALE OF TWO CITIES

This musical adaptation of *A Tale of Two Cities* was first performed at the Thameside Youth Theatre, Grays, Essex, on 25th January 1990, with the following cast:

Mme Defarge	Sarah Hicks
Defarge	Mark O'Gorman
Sydney Carton	Richard Hughes
Lucie Manette	Louise Stitt
Charles Darnay	Jamie Hughes
Dr Manette	Joe Cann
Miss Pross	Liz Beezley
Ladybird Manette	Sara Row
Barsad	Max Barber
Stryver } **French Prosecutor** }	Sean Steele
President } **English Prosecutor** }	David Giles
D'Evrémonde	Bart Pepper
Judge	Paul Dudley
Jerry Cruncher	Stuart Risby
First Peasant	Aimee Wood
Second Peasant	Anna Edwards
Third Peasant	Sarah Scott
Seamstress	Julie Challis
Jarvis Lorry } **Captain** }	John Holtom
Barmaid	Nikkie Laban

Soldiers Barry Austin, Martin Avis, Paul Dudley, David Giles, John Holtom, Bart Pepper, Francois Roypan, Sean Steele, Gary Woolf

Aristocrats Donna Abbott, Julie Challis, David Giles, Verna O'Grady, Joanne Smith, Bart Pepper, Robert Hardy

The *Gorgon's Head* Karen Barfield, Louise Bodell, Catherine Hamilton, Hannah Hogan, John Holtom, Nikkie Laban, Sarah Pacey, Julie Pollard, Lisa Pollard, Stuart Risby, Francois Roypan, Gary Woolf, Alison Spencer

Peasants Donna Abbott, Michael Adeleke, Kirsten Ashkettle, Barry Austin, Karen Barfield, Kerry Barker, Marie Barker, Karen Beadle, Jo Beesley, Cheryl Beven, Louise Bodell, Louise Brosan, Claire Brosan, Keely Cameron, Julie Challis, Dawn Cheshire, Katherine Chitty, Leah Chitty, Sheree Cook, Michelle Cowan, Emma Crompton, Louise Crompton, Karen Dellow, Susie Emms, Gemma Farr, Clarisa Ford, Natasha Fowler, Claire Freeman, Catherine Hamilton, Laura Harbourne, Sarah Head, Terri Hills, Hannah Hogan, Nikkie Laban, Kate Martin, Hilary Martin, Nicola Morant, Claire North, Wendy O'Donoghue, Verna O'Grady, Donna Oakwell, Ben Oliver, Sarah Pacey, Julie Pollard, Lisa Pollard, Helen Puzey, Ginning Ray, Stuart Risby, Francois Roypan, Anne Sage, Lucy Saunders, Joanne Smith, Nicola Smith, Alison Spencer, Nick Spencer, Sean Steele, Mark Washbourne, Ian White, Gary Woolf

PRINCIPAL CHARACTERS

Defarge, wine vendor and revolutionary
Mme Defarge, his wife
Charles Darnay, nephew to the Marquis d'Evrémonde
Lucie Manette, Dr Manette's daughter
Miss Pross, Lucie's companion
Dr Alexandre Manette, a prisoner in the Bastille
Sydney Carton, an English lawyer

SMALLER ROLES

(which may be played by members of the Chorus)

First Child, Gaspard's son
Marquis d'Evrémonde
Barsad, d'Evrémonde's spy
Stryver, Darnay's defence lawyer
Sarah, barmaid at the Gorgon's Head
Ladybird, Lucie's daughter
Prosecutor at the Old Bailey
Judge at the Old Bailey
Jerry Cruncher, an informer
Captain of Guards
Prosecutor at the French Tribunal
President of the French Tribunal
Seamstress

SYNOPSIS OF SCENES

The action takes place in Paris and London in the years from 1789

ACT I

PROLOGUE

ACT II

EPILOGUE

MUSICAL NUMBERS

ACT I

Music 1	Voice-over	
Music 2	A Tale of Two Cities	Soloist and Company
Music 3	You Never Cared Enough	Peasants and Defarge
Music 4	Gathering Storm Clouds	Defarge, Mme Defarge and Peasants
Music 5	A Tale of Two Cities (*Reprise*)	Instrumental
Music 6	Gathering Storm Clouds (*Reprise*)	Instrumental
Music 7	You Never Cared Enough (*Reprise*)	Instrumental
Music 8	Recalled to Love	Dr Manette and Lucie
Music 9	A Tale of Two Cities (*Reprise*)	Instrumental
Music 10	You Never Cared Enough (*Reprise*)	Instrumental
Music 11	Madame Guillotine	Instrumental
Music 12	The Trust in Us	Defarge, Mme Defarge and Peasants
Music 13	Different Destinations	Defarge and Mme Defarge
Music 14	Madame Guillotine	Instrumental
Music 15	The Gorgon's Head	Carton and Customers
Music 16	The Looking Glass	Carton
Music 17	The Nobles' Minuet	D'Evrémonde and Aristocrats
Music 18	Gathering Storm Clouds (*Reprise*)	Instrumental
Music 19	I Wonder What I'd Do	Darnay and Lucie
Music 20	I Wonder What I'd Do (*Reprise*)	Carton, Darnay and Lucie
Music 21	Gathering Storm Clouds (*Reprise*)	Instrumental
Music 22	Gathering Storm Clouds (*Reprise*)	Mme Defarge, Defarge, Gaspard, Peasants

ACT II

Music 23	This Time For Us	Defarge, Mme Defarge, Peasants
Music 24	A Tale of Two Cities (*Reprise*)	Instrumental
Music 25	You Must Go, My Friend	Instrumental
Music 26	Madame Guillotine	Peasants
Music 27	I Wonder What I'd Do (*Reprise*)	Instrumental
Music 28	I Wonder What I'd Do (*Reprise*)	Lucie

Music 29	This Time For Us (*Reprise*)	Instrumental
Music 30	A Chance To Love	Instrumental
Music 31	The Looking Glass (*Reprise*)	Instrumental
Music 32	The Looking Glass (*Reprise*)	Carton
Music 33	Drums in La Forge	Instrumental
Music 34	You Must Go, My Friend	Carton
Music 35	You Must Go, My Friend (*Reprise*)	Carton
Music 36	Madame Guillotine (*Reprise*)	Instrumental
Music 37	A Chance To Love (*Reprise*) Mme Defarge, Miss Pross, Defarge	
Music 38	A Chance To Love (*Reprise*)	Instrumental
Music 39	A Tale of Two Cities (*Reprise*)	Company

The Vocal Score and Orchestral Parts for this play are available from Samuel French Ltd

ACT I

Darkness

Music 1

Eerie sounds can be heard; they continue under the following voice-over

Voice It was the best of times, it was the worst of times. It was the spring of hope, it was the winter of despair. We were all going direct to Heaven, we were all going direct the other way. We had everything before us, we had nothing before us   in short, the period was very much like the present ...

A spotlight comes up on the Soloist

Music 2: A Tale of Two Cities

Soloist   It's just a tale of two cities
Maybe yours or maybe mine;
A tale of the people
From some other time.
A lady loved, loved by two
And how others could feel;
An ageing shoemaker
Locked in the Bastille.

Chorus   Enter any great city
When every soul is asleep.
Can you imagine all the secrets they must keep?
Well, the strangest of strangers —
When you look it's so true
Is no stranger, stranger than you.

During the second verse, the rest of the cast enter and and take up positions on stage

Soloist   It's just a tale of foolishness
                   That caused misery and grief,
                   Leaving words of wisdom
                   In a sea of disbelief.
                   It was a dream filled with promise
                   That came to the light
                   Only to discover
                   It was shattered in the fight.

The rest of the cast harmonize quietly with the last chorus

Chorus   Enter any great city
                   When every soul is asleep.
                   Can you imagine all the secrets they must keep?
                   Well, the strangest of strangers —
                   When you look it's so true
                   Is no stranger, stranger than you.
                   Stranger than you,
                   Stranger than you,
                   Stranger than you.

SCENE 1

France

A bustling street scene

The exterior of Defarge's wine shop stands L; outside it is a table surrounded by stools. Market traders are plying their wares and children are playing noisily around them. Mme Defarge, who is knitting, Gaspard and two Peasants are sitting around the table, talking amongst themselves. The First Child, Gaspard's son, aged about seven, is pulling at Gaspard's sleeve, trying to get his attention

Gaspard (*relenting*) All right, all right, but just *once more* and that's all.

Gaspard picks up the First Child by an arm and a leg and swings him round a couple of times, then puts him down and returns to the table. The First Child steals Gaspard's grey beret from his belt and runs R, followed at speed by Gaspard

Defarge enters R, *carrying further supplies of wine*

The First Child collides with Defarge

Defarge Hey, be careful.
Gaspard Yes, be careful, we don't want to lose the wine.
Defarge You drink a lot faster than you move, Gaspard.
Gaspard I'll move when the time comes, Defarge, when the time comes.
Mme Defarge And may that day come soon.

All at the table agree

Defarge (*putting the wine supplies down on the table*) Let's drink to that.

Gaspard reaches across, takes the beret from the First Child and then puts it on the Child's head, jokingly pulling it over his eyes

Gaspard Go play, we've got things to discuss. (*He returns to the table*)

The discussion around the table continues, becoming slightly conspiratorial. The sound of an approaching carriage can be heard off R

The First Child, chased by another child, runs off R

There is a thud, off — the carriage has hit something   then a scream

The Child that chased the First Child runs on, into the arms of its mother

Gaspard runs off R, *then returns carrying the First Child in his arms*

Defarge clears the wine shop table and Gaspard puts the First Child on it. Mme Defarge tends to the boy, mopping up his blood with the beret, which is now blood red

Darnay enters R

Mme Defarge The child is dead.
Gaspard He is dead ... they've killed my child.
Darnay Oh, my God.

The Marquis d' Evrémonde, Barsad and a Coachman enter

D'Evrémonde What's all this fuss?
Darnay (*sharply*) Our carriage has just run over a child, Uncle.
D'Evrémonde Oh, how tiresome.
Darnay Tiresome? Have you no feelings whatever?

D' Evrémonde looks to Barsad and stifles a yawn

Gaspard Killed ... killed.
Defarge Be brave, my dear Gaspard. It is better the poor little plaything to die so, than to live. It has died in a moment without pain; could it have lived an hour so happily?
D'Evrémonde Ah, a philosopher. How do they call you?
Defarge Defarge.
D'Evrémonde Of what trade?
Defarge Vendor of wine. Here is my shop.
D'Evrémonde Well, philosopher, vendor of wine, can you not stop this fool from making such a scene?
Defarge It was his child that was killed.
D'Evrémonde And it is no wonder. You people are always in the way. How do I know what injuries have been done to my horse? Here, take this and give it to the father. (*He throws a coin on the floor*) Spend it as you will. (*He moves to leave*)
Gaspard (*lunging towards d' Evrémonde*) I don't want your money, you cur.

Defarge restrains Gaspard and holds Gaspard's head to his chest

D'Evrémonde (*turning slowly to face Gaspard*) What did you say?
Defarge He said "God bless you, sir."
D'Evrémonde Tell that fool, when he calms himself, that he owes his life to your quick wit. (*To Darnay*) Come, Charles, we have spent enough time with this rabble.

D' Evrémonde, Barsad and the Coachman exit R

Defarge God bless you, sir, God bless you.

Darnay (*looking towards the table, trying to offer help*) I'm sorry ... is there anything I ...? Please forgive us ... I'm so sorry ...

Mme Defarge stares at him

At a loss for words, Darnay exits R

Gaspard (*breaking away from Defarge*) You blessed him. You blessed the killer of my child.

Defarge Blessed him? As God is my witness I'd kill him with my own hands. (*He pauses*) But it is not the time. Our time will come. (*He picks up the coin*) At this moment, I'd bless the *Devil* to his face! (*He throws the coin off* R)

Music 3: You Never Cared Enough

Peasants   When did you go out in the cold?
When did you think about the old?
When did the sorrow ever show in your eyes?
You never cared enough
When will you care enough to cry?

When did you face a hungry day?
When did you feel the need to pray?
When did you never have a warm place to lie?
You never cared enough
When will you care enough to cry?

Musical break

When did you feel another's hurt?
When did your soft hands touch the dirt?
When did you want something that you couldn't buy?
You never cared enough —
When will you care enough to cry?

Defarge   We trod the grape, you drank the wine;
We stood in rags, your clothes were fine.
The things we loved, you took them all:
Our lives a waste, your life was full.

> A man is just a man for what he is
> And not for what he has.

Peasants   When did you hear our tiny voice?
When did you leave us any choice?
When will you see that every bird needs to fly?
You never cared enough
When will you care enough to cry?

> When did you go out in the cold?
> When did you think about the old?
> When did the sorrow ever show in your eyes?
> You never cared enough
> When will you care enough to cry?

Defarge (*speaking*) Fear not, patriots. Although this child's heart beats no more, within our minds we must uphold his youth. The innocence of a child and the anger of a nation will ease the pain. We will toast our victory in his memory and the memory of other patriots who, alas, will not share with us in the time of reckoning. Go now, citizens, and shed no tears. We must conserve our energy, for our time is coming.

Music 4: Gathering Storm Clouds

The Peasants leave the stage while singing the opening chorus, leaving Defarge and Mme Defarge alone on stage for the following verse

Peasants   Gathering storm clouds,
Gathering storm clouds,
Gathering storm clouds,
Gathering storm clouds.

Defarge   ⎫ Look well upon that broken doll.
Mme Defarge ⎬ They've crushed his body, not his soul.
The blade they use to pull our strings
Will soon be used for other things.

> His tiny life will leave a spark
> To lead us when the path grows dark.
> The wind of change has started blowing;
> We've lost a seed but we're still growing.

Gathering storm clouds,
Gathering storm clouds,
Gathering storm clouds,
This kind of reign will never happen again.

Music 5: A Tale of Two Cities (*Reprise*)

SCENE 2

France. A road outside Paris. A short time later

The stage is completely empty. The Lights come up on the DR *area only*

D'Evrémonde, Barsad , Darnay and a Soldier enter R

D'Evrémonde Charles, why do you carry on so? Lives such as theirs are cheap.
Darnay Lives such as ours are cheap, Uncle. Throughout France, our family is looked upon with fear and contempt.
D'Evrémonde Detestation of the high is the involuntary homage of the low. You must uphold the family honour, Charles.
Darnay Honour? How can you speak of honour after what happened today?
D'Evrémonde (*flippantly*) Nothing happened.
Darnay You call a human life nothing?
D'Evrémonde These people aren't human, no more than any animal that lives in the dirt and filth is human.
Darnay But don't you realize it's our system that perpetuates the dirt and filth, as you call it.
D'Evrémonde System? I haven't any system, Charles. I just eat and drink and try to enjoy myself as much as possible. (*He turns to Barsad; laughing*) There's no system to it.
Darnay We have done wrong and will soon reap the fruits of vengeance. I cannot be a part of it any longer. I shall leave behind the d'Evrémonde honour and make a new life for myself   in England.
D'Evrémonde By what means, may I ask?
Darnay By my own labour. Goodbye, Uncle. May we never meet again.

Darnay exits L

D'Evrémonde (*calling after him*) Be careful, Charles, I hear they do not like spies in England. (*To Barsad*) I hope I can rely on you to take care of this little matter.
Barsad Of course.

Barsad exits L. *D'Evrémonde and the Soldier exit* R

Music 6: Gathering Storm Clouds (*Reprise*)

SCENE 3

France. Inside Defarge's wine shop and inside Dr Manette's workshop

The wine shop is set C, *with stools and tables at which several Peasants are sitting; others mill around them. Defarge and Mme Defarge sit* C

The Lights come up C

On a rostrum UR, *Dr Manette sits at his workbench, making ladies' shoes. As the scene begins this area of the stage is in darkness*

Lucie Manette, Mr Lorry and Miss Pross enter the wine shop from R

Lorry Monsieur Defarge?
Defarge (*indifferently*)That is my name.
Lorry My name is Jarvis Lorry. We have come to collect Dr Manette.
Defarge (*recognizing Mr Lorry and moving forward to shake his hand*)Ah, but of course. I received your letter. How was your journey? (*He nods towards Lucie*) Is this the daughter?
Lorry This is Lucie, yes.
Defarge (*nodding a greeting and studying Lucie's face*) I was your father's servant for many years.
Lucie I know. Mr Lorry has explained everything to me. I wish to thank you for caring for my father since his release from the Bastille.
Defarge Your father was a good man.
Lucie Was? Is he greatly changed?
Defarge Changed? He is destroyed!

Lucie lowers her head, upset

Miss Pross (*moving forward to console Lucie; to Defarge*) Please Monsieur, try to be aware of Miss Manette's feelings.

Defarge (*touching Lucie's arm, softening*) I am sorry. Perhaps with your love there is still some hope for him.

Lucie Can we go to him?

Defarge Yes, he is in the garret room over the shop.

Miss Pross Is he alone?

Defarge He is as alone as when they first released him to my care, alone within himself. I will take Lucie to him. You must not be shocked by what you see.

Lorry Do you not allow him to join you here?

Defarge It cannot be so.

Miss Pross Why ever not?

Defarge Because he has lived so long locked up, he might come to I know not what harm, were it any different.

Lorry It is possible, I suppose.

Defarge (*to Lucie*) Come, I will take you to him.

Music 7: You Never Cared Enough (*Reprise*)

Defarge leads Lucie towards Dr Manette's workshop UR. The Lights cross-fade to the workshop as Defarge and Lucie pass across the stage. Dr Manette is working at his bench as Defarge and Lucie come into the workshop

Defarge Dr Manette ... Doctor ... There's someone here to see you.

Lucie moves forward and Dr Manette shies back into his chair

Lucie What's wrong? Does he fear me?

Defarge He's confused. He sees not you, but his wife   your mother.

Lucie Father. (*She reaches for him*) I have come to take you home. (*She looks back at Defarge, as if asking him for time alone with her father*)

Defarge I will take his belongings to Mr Lorry. (*He collects Dr Manette's bag and returns to the wine shop*)

Lucie (*kneeling by Dr Manette*) Father, I am here. You are safe now.

Music 8: Recalled To Love

Dr Manette   Her face, it's the same but it couldn't be.
                   Look at me.
                   Her eyes are as bright but they shouldn't shine.
                   Look at mine.

Her hair is still as gold,
She feels as warm as I am cold.
It's my mind trying to find what what I can't hold.

Her voice is the same, like a melody,
A memory;
The way she spoke my name keeps coming back to me,
Constantly.
Like a flower-scented breeze
Drifts among the lonely trees,
So my mind tries to find what I can't hold.

Chorus   Recalled to love,
Recalled to life,
Recalled to light,
Out of the dark and lonely night.
Recalled to me, recalled to you,
Try to recall the things we knew.

Lucie   I never knew that you existed.
I thought you died when I was young.
But oh, I've heard so much about you, ooh ooh,
That now I love you just as strong.

Lucie sings the chorus

Dr Manette   Her face, it's the same, but it couldn't be.
Look at me.
Her eyes are as bright but they shouldn't shine.
Look at mine.
Her hair is still as gold,
She feels as warm as I am cold;
It's my mind trying to find what I can't hold.

Lucie helps Dr Manette to his feet and supports him as they head for the door They proceed slowly down the stairs, reaching the wine shop area as the song ends

Lucie   Although my love cannot be her love,
I'll give you all the love I own,

> And I will lead you, lead you to the sunshine, ooh ooh,
> For I have come to take you home.

They sing the chorus. Lucie and Dr Manette walk into the wine shop. The Lights cross-fade to the wine shop. Miss Pross and Mr Lorry move to attend Lucie and Dr Manette as Mme Defarge addresses the assembled Peasants

Mme Defarge Citizens, patriots!

All the Peasants turn and listen

> What further proof do we need of the evil that we allow to fester in France? This good doctor was locked away in the Bastille for sixteen years.

The crowd murmurs its shock

> His crime was to condemn an aristocrat for the rape and murder of a girl he had tried to save. Take a good look at this man, patriots, and remember. (*To Lucie*) Take him back to England and release him from his pain.

Lorry (*shaking hands with Defarge and Mme Defarge*) Thank you Madame, Monsieur Defarge.

Lucie (*taking Madame Defarge's hand*) How can I ever thank you?

Mme Defarge Always take pride in the Manette name. Your father is a brave and fine man. Go now, he has his freedom.

Lucie, Lorry, Miss Pross and Dr Manette exit

Defarge (*putting his hand in his pocket and pulling out Dr Manette's diary*) I must give Dr Manette his diary.

Mme Defarge No. (*She restrains Defarge, takes the diary from him and puts it in her apron*) We will keep it.

Defarge Why?

Mme Defarge It is just as much our memory as it is his. He is free now, we must still fight for our freedom.

The Lights fade to Black-out

Music 9: A Tale of Two Cities (*Reprise*)

SCENE 4

England. Inside Sydney Carton's house

The room and the chairs and table in it are strewn with wine bottles. There is a pile of legal documents on the table

Carton, who bears a striking resemblance to Charles Darnay, is sitting alone, drinking

Stryver enters, removing his coat

Stryver Well, Carton, have you done any work on the treason case?
Carton (*not looking up*) I've been working all night.
Stryver (*clearing bottles from a chair so that he can lay his coat on it*) You've been drinking all night.
Carton It's the same thing.
Stryver (*pacing nervously up and down*) Mr Lorry has contacted me personally and has asked that I put all my energies into this case.
Carton Go ahead ... (*He pours himself another drink*) You would do well with such a delicate case. Your acting expertise would be most beneficial.
Stryver What are your drunken ramblings now, Carton?
Carton You work off other people's scripts, don't you?
Stryver I don't pay you to be insolent.
Carton No, you pay for my legal expertise.
Stryver Carton, just look over the brief, please. You will do well out of it.
Carton *You* will, you mean. (*He picks the brief up off the desk*)
Stryver Carton, just look at it and try to do your best.
Carton (*looking up at Stryver*) My best is as good as any other man's, I believe. (*He starts to read the brief and becomes more absorbed in it*)

There is a pause. Stryver resumes his pacing, occasionally looking across at Carton

Stryver Well? Any ideas?

Carton The chief witness, Barsad, appears a little dubious. I'll ask Jerry to put his ear to the ground. (*He puts down the brief and reaches for his glass*)

Stryver You shouldn't mix with such slovenly and careless characters.

Carton Most of your memorable victories were aided by slovenly and careless characters.

Stryver (*picking up his coat and placing it over his arm*) I only came to see how far you'd got. I must go now; I have an important meeting to attend.

Carton Oh, please, don't let me delay you.

Stryver Try to minimize the drinking, Sydney.

Carton looks set to call out

Stryver exits

Carton Try to look in the looking-glass occasionally, *Mister* Stryver.

Music 10: You Never Cared Enough (*Reprise*)

SCENE 5

England. A courtroom inside the Old Bailey

The Judge, Prosecutor Stryver and Carton sit C, facing the audience. Darnay is in the dock. Lucie is in the witness box, R, with Dr Manette, Miss Pross and Mr Lorry nearby, watching the proceedings. Barsad is L, waiting his turn to give evidence

Prosecutor Miss Manette. Have you ever been to France?

Lucie Yes, sir.

Prosecutor Could you briefly tell the court on what purpose?

Lucie My father, Dr Manette, was a prisoner in the Bastille for many years. After hearing of his release from his former servant Monsieur Defarge, I went there with Miss Pross and Mr Lorry to bring him home. He was too ill to make the journey on his own.

Prosecutor Miss Manette. Have you ever seen the prisoner before?

Lucie Yes, sir.

Prosecutor Where?

Lucie On board the package ship from Calais.
Prosecutor Miss Manette, did you see the prisoner pass documents to two
  French gentlemen?
Lucie Mr Darnay was very kind to my father.
Prosecutor Miss Manette, please answer the question.
Lucie (*quietly*) Yes.
Judge Please speak up, Miss Manette.
Lucie Yes, but I must say that Mr Darnay helped my father and me. He was
  very kind to us.
Prosecutor Thank you Miss Manette. No further questions. (*He sits*)
Stryver (*standing*) No questions, my Lord. (*He sits*)
Judge You may sit down, Miss Manette.
Prosecutor I call Mr John Barsad.

*Lucie returns to her seat (with Miss Pross and her party) and Barsad takes
the witness stand*

Have you ever seen the prisoner before?
Barsad Yes, sir, on three different occasions.
Prosecutor Did the prisoner, on any of these occasions, act suspiciously?
Barsad Yes, sir. I clearly saw the prisoner pass secret documents to two
  French gentlemen on each occasion.
Prosecutor How can you be sure they were government documents?
Barsad I have worked for the British government on several occasions.
  I have dealt with many a security matter involving sensitive issues. The
  documents passed between these gentlemen were definitely British and
  secret.

Jerry Cruncher enters L

*He beckons to Carton, who moves over to speak to him. The Lights fade
on Barsad and the Prosecutor during the following exchange so that
attention focuses on Carton and Jerry Cruncher*

Prosecutor Please, Mr Barsad, would you kindly tell the court about the
  work that you have done with our government.
Barsad For several years I have been employed by the government as ...
  (*His voice fades but he continues "talking" in mime*)
Carton Well, Jerry, my good fellow. What have you for me today?

Jerry Cruncher The man Barsad works for the French. He has been paid
to give evidence against the prisoner.
Carton By whom has he been paid?
Jerry Cruncher That's not important. The usual price.
Carton Of course. (*He hands Jerry a coin*)
Jerry Cruncher (*taking the coin, flipping it in the air and pocketing it*)
Just say his real name: Soloman. He'll soon change his mind. (*He hands
Carton a piece of paper*)
Carton Are you sure?
Jerry Cruncher I'm sure. Just say his real name.
Carton Thank you, my good man, you've been most helpful.
Jerry Cruncher Will we see you tonight? (*He mimes tipping a tankard*)
Carton (*positively*) Of course.

Jerry Cruncher exits L

*The Lights come up on the courtroom. Carton returns to his seat and hands
Stryver the paper given to him by Jerry Cruncher*

Barsad (*his voice becoming audible again*) ... so you see, my Lord, I
cannot be mistaken.

*Carton and Stryver become engrossed in a whispered conversation,
Carton indicating the prisoner then himself, with his gestures. Stryver
looks at the prisoner and at Carton, then nods in agreement*

Prosecutor (*to Barsad*) Mr Barsad, do you realize that you are accusing
the prisoner of treason?
Barsad I do, sir.
Prosecutor Thank you, Mr Barsad. Your witness, Mr Stryver.

Stryver deep in conversation, does not hear

Judge Mr Stryver.

Stryver looks up

(*Sarcastically*) If we're not interrupting anything? Your witness, Mister
Stryver ...

Stryver Thank you, m'lud. (*To Barsad*) Mr Barsad, you say you've worked for the British government?

Barsad Yes, sir.

Stryver Well, I'm sure everyone here at court is very grateful for your services to the British government, and especially for your vigilant observations.

Barsad I try to keep my eyes open, just as any loyal citizen would ——

Stryver (*interrupting him*) I'm sure you *try*, but do you always succeed?

Barsad (*bewildered*) I'm sorry?

Stryver Well, for example, did you ever see anybody very like the prisoner?

Barsad Not so alike that I could be mistaken, sir.

Stryver Look well upon that gentleman, my learned friend there —— (*He indicates to Carton to stand up*)

Carton stands

—— and then look upon the prisoner. Mr Carton, would you be so kind as to remove your wig.

Carton removes his wig. All present gasp with amazement

How do you say? Are they very like each other? Allowing, of course, for my learned friend being a touch *slovenly* and *careless* in both his manner and appearance.

Barsad I agree there is a similarity but not so that I would be mistaken.

Stryver Please look carefully, Soloman. They are very alike, are they not, Soloman?

Judge The witness's name is Barsad.

Stryver Oh, yes, forgive me, sir. Mr Barsad, are you sure of your identification?

Barsad (*faintly*) No.

Stryver Speak up, sir.

Barsad No.

Stryver So the man you saw passing documents could have been someone else?

Barsad (*faintly*) It could have been.

Stryver Please let the court hear your answer.

Barsad (*angrily*) It could have been another man.

Stryver Thank you, Mr Barsad. (*To the Judge*) My Lord, I hereby rest my case.

Judge I have no other option than to rule that the case against Charles Darnay be dismissed due to the lack of evidence.

Barsad exits L

The Judge and Prosecutor exit R

Dr Manette, Lucie, Miss Pross and Mr Lorry move C *to join Darnay and Stryver Carton collects up his papers*

Darnay (*to Stryver*) How can I express my gratitude to you, Mr Stryver?

Stryver makes a pleasantly dismissive gesture

(*Turning to Lucie*) And, of course, thank *you*, Miss Manette. (*He kisses her hand, then turns to Dr Manette*) My deepest regrets, sir, that you and your lovely daughter became involved.

Dr Manette My dear Mr Darnay, I am just glad that justice has prevailed. We must thank Mr Stryver for his excellent defence.

Stryver I have done my best for Mr Darnay and my best is as good as any other man's, I believe.

Dr Manette I wish to invite you all to dinner at my house. We will hold the meal in honour of Mr Stryver.

Stryver Thank you, sir.

Carton (*joining the group*) I do not wish to interrupt your appreciation party, Mr Stryver, but, if anyone is interested, I will be at the *Gorgon's Head* I humbly invite you all to join me later so that we can celebrate over a bottle of fine red wine.

Miss Pross I do not believe that a public house is really the place for a young lady.

Carton But, my dear lady, I think you would find the surroundings most suitable.

Lucie (*intervening, with a mischievous look*) It will be our pleasure to meet you there, is that not so, Father?

Miss Pross looks disgusted

Dr Manette (*registering his daughter's mood; to Carton*) Of course.

Stryver (*to Carton*) We will see you after dinner.

Carton gazes at Lucie in admiration of her beauty

All but Carton leave L

He stands C, *watching them depart*

Music 11: Madame Guillotine (*Reprise*)

SCENE 6

France. Inside Defarge's wine shop

The set is the same as that for Scene 3, but the workshop does not need to be visible

A meeting is in progress; a crowd of Peasants is gathered around Defarge and Mme Defarge. Gaspard is among the crowd

Defarge Is everyone here?
Gaspard We're here and ready to go!
Mme Defarge I will lead the women.
Peasants (*cheering*) Yes!
Defarge (*raising his arms to control the crowd*) Patience! Patience! The time is *soon*.
Gaspard Why must we wait? We are ready now!
Peasants Yes!
Defarge (*quietening the crowd again*) Our patience will be the aristocrats' fall!
Mme Defarge It's all here! (*She holds up her knitting*) Each stitch removes an hour from their lives.
Peasants (*shouting louder than ever before*) Yes!

Music 12: The Trust In Us

Defarge ⎱ The time is soon,
Mme Defarge ⎰ No more to fear.

Our time of justice and of freedom is so near.
I trust in you, you trust in me,
We trust in us
We trust in France and what's to be.

All   So lean on me,
I'll lean on you.
The clouds will break, the storm will pass,
The day's anew.
Together we will be as one,
Don't look behind, look straight ahead,
Your life's begun.

The time is soon,
No more to fear
Our time of justice and of freedom is so near.
I trust in you, you trust in me,
We trust in us,
We trust in France and what's to be.

*During the following instrumental verse and the last chorus, the
Peasants slowly leave the stage*

The time is soon,
No more to fear,
Our time of justice and of freedom is so near.
I trust in you, you trust in me,
We trust in love and laughter,
Life and Liberty.

Defarge and Mme Defarge are alone

Defarge Our dream is to be realized. Soon France will be free. Our people
will live without fear or hate.
Mme Defarge We can never forget. Our lives have been torn and our
hearts ravaged with torment. There is no miracle that will cure us of our
pain; even time cannot heal those wounds.
Defarge But in time we will learn to relax. Our bitterness will fade and
allow us to see a new life in front of us.

Mme Defarge We must revenge the life now before thinking of beginning the next.

Defarge I like to think. I yearn for the day I can take you in my arms and hold you with no anger in my heart.

Mme Defarge Always the romantic.

Defarge Please, just for tonight, can we not put our worries aside and be together as husband and wife should be?

Mme Defarge No, I need to think.

Defarge Now who's the thinker?

Mme Defarge My thoughts are of strength, yours are of a weaker kind.

Defarge Love is weak?

Mme Defarge For what we have to do, emotions such as these would only harm our cause.

Defarge We must not forget us. (*He holds her by her arms*) Together we will find a much greater power.

Mme Defarge (*earnestly pleading*) Each individual must revenge their own souls. (*She pauses, then breaks away from him*) I must leave now, I have many things to plan.

The Lights fade on the wine shop and two spots pick out Defarge and Mme Defarge

Music 13: Different Destinations

Defarge

While our world is still small,
Before we've given it all,
Let us lie with each other once more.
And though I'll try to pretend,
I'm still afraid in the end
We are leaving too much to fate to be sure.

Chorus

We never had to ask directions
On this road we've tried to pave,
And so far we've been lucky
To be going the same way.
But now I've got the strangest feeling,
I'm afraid I can't pretend,
We'll find different destinations
When our road comes to an end.

In the forthcoming days
We'll get lost in the maze
And who can say if we'll find a way through:
And though it seems that our aims
Will never quite be the same
I've got the same aspirations as you.

Repeat chorus

Mme Defarge   Please don't touch me tonight
If you're hoping to find
Anything with the slightest resemblance of love
Anywhere in my mind.
Don't touch me tonight,
Now I need to be strong,
Now I need to retain every memory of pain
I have carried so long.

You won't reach me tonight
Though I'll lay close to you.
I have so far to go that my body and soul
Cannot rest 'til I'm through.
Don't touch me tonight,
For your soft tender words
Wouldn't have the effect that a lover expects
And would just pass unheard,
If you touch me tonight.

Repeat chorus twice

Black-out

Music 14: Madame Guillotine

SCENE 7

England. Inside the Gorgon's Head *public house*

There are two tables in the room, laden with bottles and tankards and surrounded by stools

Sarah, the barmaid, is busy serving the many drunken Customers, among whom is Carton

Customer Come on, Sydney, give us a song!

Music 15: The *Gorgon's Head*

Carton   We're at the *Gorgon's Head* tonight,
Just drink your beer, don't start a fight,
'Cause anybody that ever saw
The room go spinning round
Will know exactly what I mean,
Will know just what I've found.

All   Here's to the *Gorgon's Head* tonight,
After a few we'll feel all right.
You won't find a better place
In the whole of London town,
You'll only see a happy face
You'll never find a frown.

Sarah   We're at the *Gorgon's Head* tonight,
You'll see it in a different light.
You don't have to worry, boy,
If you fall upon the floor
Nobody will step on you
Of that you can be sure.

Dr Manette, Lucie, Mr Lorry, Miss Pross, Stryver and Darnay enter L

Carton and the Customers dance during the following chorus, watched by the newcomers

Carton   }   We're at the *Gorgon's Head* tonight ,
Customers }   Just drink your beer, don't start a fight,

'Cause anybody that ever saw
The room go spinning round
Will know exactly what I mean,
Will know just what I've found.
We're at the *Gorgon's Head* tonight,
We're at the *Gorgon's Head* tonight.

Carton and the dancers fall to the floor Carton, seeing Dr Manette and his party, gets up and moves over to them, inadvertently dropping his wig on the floor

Carton Good-day, my fellow beings. (*He turns towards Sarah, his back to Dr Manette's party*) Sarah, a large carafe of the finest red. We come to celebrate this lucky gentleman's escape from the world beyond.
Sarah Be with you in a minute, darlin' (*She moves to collect the wine and goblets*)

Lucie picks up Carton's fallen wig and stands hesitantly waiting for the right moment to return it to him. Dr Manette and his party sit in a semi-circle L

(*Carrying wine and goblets to Dr Manette's group*) Here we are, Sydney. On the slate, I presume?
Carton My good woman, I wish not to disappoint you by breaking routine.

Sarah laughs and retires. Carton pours himself a goblet of wine and the others follow suit

A toast. Now who can I toast? It's there on the tip of my tongue.
Darnay Mr Stryver?
Carton No, no, no. Not Mr Stryver. (*He faces Lucie*) Miss Manette.

They all raise their glasses. Lucie is embarrassed by Carton's stare

Lorry I suggest we toast Mr Stryver, for, without his expertise, poor Mr Darnay would not be gracing us with his company now.

They all toast Stryver except Carton, who just raises his glass half-heartedly and pours himself another drink

Lucie Mr Stryver, why did Mr Barsad change his story?

Stryver (*slightly uncomfortable*) Well, he ——

Carton He was a spy for the French government. You learn such information by mixing with slovenly and careless company.

Stryver Yes, that's right. (*He begins to stammer nervously*) He was a ... s-s-s-spy for the French government.

Carton smirks

Darnay Well, once again I thank you for my life, good sir.

Carton Yes, I'm sure Mr Stryver has had more than enough thanks. (*To Darnay*) Now tell me, Mr Darnay. What do you intend to do?

Darnay I plan to teach French, here in England.

Carton (*raising his voice in the way drunks do*) Perhaps Miss Manette will be your first pupil?

Darnay (*tenderly*) That would indeed be a pleasure.

Lucie and Darnay gaze at each other

Carton (*sighing, aside*) Indeed it would.

During the following conversation Lucie and Darnay move away from the group, becoming engrossed in a private conversation

Customer Come on, Sydney, let's have some entertainment.

Carton Why not?

The Customers noisily encourage Carton to sing them a song

Miss Pross I believe we have had enough entertainment for this evening.

The Customers hear this and react with shouts and laughter

Carton (*to Miss Pross*) Why? Do you not wish to dance with me? (*He moves towards Miss Pross as if to manhandle her*)

Miss Pross (*backing off, with a look of disgust*) No I don't, and kindly keep your hands to yourself.

The Customers react even more strongly to this

Carton Don't worry, madam, you're quite safe. I haven't had that much
to drink.
Stryver Come, madam, there's no talking to him when he's like this. I'll
escort you to the carriage.

Miss Pross and Stryver head for the exit L

The Customers call out various comments laden with sexual innuendo

Miss Pross and Stryver exit L

Carton (*shouting after them*) Come back Stryver, let's celebrate your
victory!
Sarah (*ringing the bell and shouting*) Time, ladies and gentlemen, time!

The Customers start to leave

Lorry Good-night, Mr Carton. Maybe you should go home, too.

Mr Lorry exits L

Dr Manette Good-night, Mr Carton. It has been an ... an interesting
evening.(*He turns away and joins Darnay and Lucie*)

*Carton sits with his back to Lucie, Darnay and Dr Manette, drinking and
slowly falling asleep. Lucie indicates to Dr Manette that she has to return
Carton's wig to its owner She walks towards Carton, leaving Darnay and
Dr Manette talking together*

Sarah shows out the last remaining Customers and exits herself

*Lucie reaches over Carton's shoulder with the wig, which tickles his face
and wakes him up*

Lucie Don't lose this ...
Carton (*taking her hand and kissing it*) Where would I be without you,
Sarah?
Lucie Mr Carton!
Carton (*rising to his feet unsteadily*) Oh, I do beg your pardon, Miss
Manette.

Lucie (*smiling, sharing the joke with him*) Under the circumstances, I think I can accept your apology.

Carton It seems the wine is a little strong tonight   or perhaps my intoxication is due to something more potent.

Lucie I can't imagine anything more potent than wine, Mr Carton.

Carton (*teasing*) Then you have obviously never looked in a looking-glass, Miss Manette ...

Lucie Oh, but I have, Mr Carton, and far too often to succumb to this kind of flattery.

Carton What a shame. Now I'll never know.

Lucie Know what, Mr Carton?

Carton (*regaining his composure*) Whether you might join me for a day's riding in the country this weekend?

Lucie I'm sorry, Mr Carton. I plan to see Mr Darnay this weekend.

Miss Pross enters L

Miss Pross Lucie, we're waiting in the carriage.

Miss Pross exits L

Lucie Goodbye Mr Carton. I hope we meet again. (*She returns to Dr Manette and Darnay*)

Carton (*watching Lucie*) Maybe some other time, perhaps ... (*He sits again and resumes his drinking, lost within himself*)

Darnay indicates to Dr Manette and Lucie that he wishes to say goodbye to Carton. He approaches Carton

Dr Manette and Lucie exit L

Darnay Good-night, Mr Carton. And thank you.

Carton Why are you thanking me?

Darnay (*slightly taken aback*) Well ... er ... for any help you gave to Mr Stryver on my behalf.

Carton The only help this slovenly drunk could give to you, Mr Darnay, is to make you look quite acceptable by comparison. (*He goes to sip his drink, stops and looks at Darnay*) Do you think I like you?

Darnay I thought so, but now I'm not so sure.

Carton I neither like you nor dislike you. I hold no emotions for anybody
and nobody holds any emotion for me. (*He studies the glass he is
holding*) A simple existence, wouldn't you say, Mr Darnay? (*He looks
up at Darnay*) Now hurry off to your new–found friend and leave me to
mine. (*He holds up his glass as if to toast Darnay*)
Darnay I'm sorry you feel this this way, Mr Carton.
Carton Don't give me your sympathy. I don't need it.
Darnay Good-night.

Darnay exits L

Carton is alone

Music 16: The Looking-Glass

Carton   I'm not searching for the future in the past;
When the morning comes I'm glad to be alive.
Though I treat every single day like it's my last
I've got faith in me, I'm sure that I'll survive.

If you ask just where in hell I'm heading for
I can lead you to a mirror on the wall,
And if you know where you're going and you're sure
Then the looking-glass is looking at a fool.

It seems the more I grow, the less I know;
The night sky makes me feel real small.
The open sea amazes me,
And the looking-glass is looking at a fool.

So remember if you spend your time just searching,
That the more you find the more you'll have to lose.
You've just got to find yourself or wind up hurting
When you see that lonely stranger in your shoes.

I have walked along both paths of love and freedom
And found that freedom can be kind when love is cruel,
But it seems I never found a thing until I lost it
When the looking-glass is looking at a fool,
When the looking-glass is looking at a fool,
When the looking-glass is looking at a fool.

SCENE 8

France. Inside the Marquis d'Evrémonde's chateau

There is a balcony L *with french doors leading off it*

A ball is in full swing. The Marquis d'Evrémonde is standing C, *surrounded by Aristocrats who are laughing at a joke he has told*

Music 17: The Nobles' Minuet

D'Evrémonde moves downstage, the Aristocrats parting before him

D'Evrémonde   We are sort of second cousins to the King
And that entitles us to almost anything,
For not just anyone at all
Gets invited to our Ball,
It's only sort of second cousins to the King.

D'Evrémonde moves to one side as the Aristocrats dance

Aristocrats   Our blood is a distinctive shade of blue
And nothing like the kind of stuff
They'll find in you.
So if we're tall and quite refined,
It's due to our generic line
Because we're sort of second cousins to the King.

Gaspard enters L *and makes his way towards the balcony, keeping out of sight of the Aristocrats. He hides on the balcony, waiting*

The Lights dim, except for a spot on Gaspard

The dance continues in slow motion during the following verse

Gaspard (*speaking*)   You are sort of second cousins to the King
And that entitles you to almost anything,
But not just anyone at all
Gets invited to this ball
It's only sort of second cousins to the King.

The Lights come up on the ballroom again

Aristocrats (*singing*)The peasants, they're the scruffy ones that smell
And keep complaining that they're not treated well,
But we've done our best at court
To make sure they're never short
Of charming sort of second cousins to the King.

The dance ends. D'Evrémonde opens the french doors and steps out on to the balcony.The Aristocrats gather in small groups, talking and laughing. Gaspard lunges forward, stabbing D'Evrémonde through the heart. Everyone freezes

Gaspard This is from the Jacquery. May you ride swiftly to your grave.

Music 18: Gathering Storm Clouds (Reprise)

SCENE 9

England. Dr Manette's garden

Dr Manette and Miss Pross are seated together on a wooden bench c; Miss Pross is winding wool from a large skein that Dr Manette is holding. Mr Lorry is with them. Lucie and Darnay stand nearby, obviously wanting to be alone together

Darnay I find it most enthralling, spending my Sundays with you ... and your family, Lucie.

Darnay and Lucie smile at his joke. Miss Pross gives them a sideways look

Lucie (*slightly louder*) Would you like to see the gardens, Charles?
Miss Pross (*without looking up*) Please stay where I can see you.
Lucie
Darnay } (*together laughing*) We will, Miss Pross.

Music 19: I Wonder What I'd Do

*Darnay and Lucie cross from c to L, watched by Miss Pross. The Lights
cross-fade to c. Lucie uses her fan to hide her coyness at Darnay's
advances, looking round at Miss Pross from time to time and then
returning her gaze to Darnay. Darnay unsettles Lucie by walking round
her as they sing*

Darnay   I wonder what I'd do
                    If I wasn't loved by you,
                    Just drift around much like the falling leaves.
                    I wonder where I'd be
                    If you weren't loving me
                    Like a sailing ship left waiting for the breeze.

                    And sometimes, when I need a place to hide
                    You call for me to come inside
                    And when I think I'm just another man,
                    You make me feel
                    So much more than I am.

Lucie   I wonder what I'd do
                    If I wasn't loved by you;
                    Just hang around and watch my life go by.
                    I wonder what I'd be
                    If you weren't loving me;
                    A lonely soul left waiting high and dry.

                    And sometimes, when I need a place to hide,
                    You call for me to come inside,
                    And when I feel I'm just another woman
                    You make me feel
                    So much more than I am.

Darnay   I wonder what I'd do, I wonder what I'd do,
                    I wonder what I'd do,
                    Without you.

They kiss and return to Dr Manette and Miss Pross

The Lights cross-fade to c

Darnay (*to Dr Manette*) Dr Manette, I ... (*He looks at Lucie*)

Lucie nods encouragingly

(*Turning back to Dr Manette*) ... I hope to have a moment with you.
Dr Manette Yes, Charles.
Darnay (*in a rush*) I wish to ask you for your daughter's hand in marriage.
Dr Manette Is Lucie happy?
Lucie Oh I am, Father, I am.
Dr Manette (*standing and shaking Darnay's hand*) Then, Charles, I would be honoured to have you as my son-in-law.

Darnay takes Dr Manette R; *Lucie moves to Miss Pross to share her excitement. The Lights cross-fade to* R

Darnay Dr Manette. There is something I must tell you.
Dr Manette Yes, Charles.
Darnay I live in England under a false identity. I left France because I despised what was happening there. I lived with my uncle, a marquis. His treatment of people disgusted me; he cared for no-one but himself. I felt shame for France and was ashamed of my family name. Because of this, I denounced my claim to any wealth or property that my uncle has and set sail for a new life in England.
Dr Manette My good Charles. You cannot choose to which family you are born. Your birth name means nothing. Warmth of the heart is far more important to me, and of course to Lucie. You are to be my son, regardless of what title you use.
Darnay (*obviously relieved*) I think I will stay with Darnay. The name D'Evrémonde repulses me.
Dr Manette (*shocked*) What ... what did you say?
Darnay D'Evrémonde. My name was Charles d'Evrémonde.

The Lights fade

Music 20: I Wonder What I'd Do (*Reprise*)

A spot comes up on Carton, L

Dr Manette, Miss Pross and Mr Lorry exit, during the first verse of the song

Darnay and Lucie move R

Carton   I wonder what I'd do
                  If I had a chance with you;
                  Perhaps my life would all become worthwhile.
                  I wonder where I'd be
                  If you ever looked at me,
                  If I could be the one to make you smile.

                  Then sometimes when I need a place to hide
                  I'd call for you to come inside,
                  But when you see me as just another man
                  It makes me see
                  The way that I am.

A spot comes up on Darnay and Lucie R

Darnay ⎫   I wonder what I'd do   Carton I love you,
Lucie ⎭   If I wasn't loved by you   I need you,
              Just drift around
              Much like the falling leaves.   I'm calling out to you.

              I wonder where I'd be   I love you,
              If you weren't loving me   I need you,
              Like a sailing ship   I know the reason why.
              Left waiting for the breeze

              Then sometimes when I need a place to hide
              You call for me to come inside,
              But when you think I'm just another (wo)man,
              It makes me see the way that I am.
              I wonder what I'd do,
              I wonder what I'd do,
              I wonder what I'd do,
              Without you.

Black-out

Music 21: Gathering Storm Clouds (*Reprise*)

SCENE 10

France. Outside the walls of the Bastille

Drumbeats

A firing squad of Soldiers is preparing for an execution, watched by groups of Aristocrats and Peasants. The Peasants are wearing red berets, the symbol of the Revolution. Mme Defarge is standing DR, *holding a pistol; Defarge is* DL

Gaspard is brought on by a group of Soldiers. They begin to prepare him for execution. When they have finished, the Captain of the Guards steps forward to give orders

Captain (*raising his arm*) Ready, aim ...
Mme Defarge (*stepping forward, raising her pistol and shooting the Captain*) Thank you for the honour, kind sir!

Before the Soldiers can react, the Peasants attack them. More Peasants appear and the battle commences

Defarge Victory for France!
Mme Defarge To the Bastille!

Music 22: Gathering Storm Clouds (*Reprise*)

More Peasants enter through the auditorium. Aristocrats attempting to escape are driven back to the battle

More soldiers enter and join the fight

Although the battle is not easy for the Peasants, and they suffer great losses, it is quite obvious that they will be the victors. Their methods are unsophisticated; they fight savagely and with euphoria, feeling their cause is justified. As the song reaches its climax, it is clear that the Peasants are the victors

Peasants   Gathering storm clouds
Gathering storm clouds
Gathering storm clouds
Gathering storm clouds.

Verse 1   Our blood will form a tidal wave
                     That sweeps them to an early grave.
                     Their bloated bodies filled with greed
                     Will lie in fields and turn to seed.
                     This whisper will become a scream,
                     That wakes this nightmare to a dream,
                     Each heart prepared to pay the price
                     And die before a compromise.

Chorus   Gathering storm clouds
                     Gathering storm clouds
                     Gathering storm clouds,
                     This kind of reign will never happen again.

                     We'll burn the things that represent
                     Their idle lives carelessly spent
                     And when the ashes cool to dust
                     We'll build anew this time for us.

Chorus

Musical break

*The battle continues; by the end of the next chorus the Soldiers are
defeated*

                     Gathering storm clouds
                     Gathering storm clouds
                     Gathering storm clouds
                     Gathering storm clouds.

*During the next verse and chorus the Peasants stand motionless, facing
the audience. Defarge and Mme Defarge move c*

*The Peasants repeat Verse 1 then divide into two groups to sing the
following*

                     Gathering storm clouds   This time for us
                     Gathering storm clouds   This time for us
                     Gathering storm clouds   This time for us
                     Gathering storm clouds.   This time for us.

Gathering storm clouds
Gathering storm clouds
Gathering storm clouds.

The Peasants strike aggressive poses and hold them until the CURTAIN *falls*

This kind of reign will never happen again.

CURTAIN

ACT II

SCENE 1

France. Outside the Bastille

As the CURTAIN *rises, there is the sound of an explosion*

The dead and dying litter the stage. Defarge is standing at the back of the stage, on a higher level, holding a flag. Among the bodies, R, a woman cradles a dead child. Madame Defarge is L, helping an injured peasant

Defarge (*screaming*) Victory!

Music 23: This Time For Us

Defarge puts his flag down and makes his way over to the woman. As he begins the following song, he picks up the body of the child and indicates to the woman to stand up too

More Peasants enter and carry away the dead

When all the bodies have been removed, the Peasants gather C, *with Defarge and Madame Defarge standing* L *and* R

Defarge   No time for tears,
Hate's paid the price
For each must give the things he loves
As sacrifice.
Stand up my friend,
Don't cry today,
Tomorrow's tears will help to wash
The blood away.

Chorus   This time for all,
No longer half.

This time each hungry soul will taste
The fatted calf.

Defarge ⎫ This time for you,
Mme Defarge ⎭ This time for me,
This time for us,
This time for France and Liberty.

All   So lean on me,
I'll lean on you.
The clouds have broken,
The storm is past,
The day's anew.
Together we will be as one;
Don't look behind,
Look straight ahead,
Your life's begun.

Repeat chorus

The echoes of
Our eager feet
Will tell a waiting world
This journey is complete.
The fallow fields
Once more will be
Given the life they've waited for
So patiently.

Let shadows fall
And go to ground.
The darkest secret in your heart
Has now been found.
At last we're free,
Free of the weight;
We'll find that love
Is so much easier than hate.

This time for all,
No longer half.
This time each hungry soul will taste
The fatted calf.

This time for you,
This time for me,
This time for love and laughter,
 Life and Liberty.

Humming the melody of the song, the Peasants leave the stage, helping the injured

Defarge and Madame Defarge walk c. Drumbeats

Defarge At last, it has come at last.
Mme Defarge But it is only the beginning.

Madame Defarge exits R

Defarge watches her go, then exits L as the music ends

Black-out

Music 24: A Tale of Two Cities (*Reprise*)

SCENE 2

England. Dr Manette's garden

Darnay, Lucie and Dr Manette are seated at a table R, on which there are a bottle of wine and glasses

Miss Pross enters R

Miss Pross Have you seen the little Ladybird? It is way past her bedtime.
Darnay Don't worry, Miss Pross. I'm sure she is in good hands.

Carton enters R carrying Ladybird, Lucie's and Darnay's daughter on his shoulders

Carton (*imitating the sound made to stop a horse*) Kind madame, this horse can go no further.

Ladybird (*protesting*) But, Uncle Sydney ... Just one more ride ... please ...
Miss Pross No, young lady. It's time for bed.
Carton (*saluting ironically and smiling*) Prossy has spoken!
Miss Pross I've told you before   (*she sarcastically emphasizes his name*)   Syd — ney   it's Miss Pross to you.
Lucie (*to the child*) Come, my precious, you must have your sleep.
Ladybird (*kissing each of the adults in turn*) Good-night, Mother. Good-night, Father. Good-night, Grandfather. Good-night   Uncle   (*she copies Miss Pross's sarcasm*) Syd   ney.

All laugh ...

... except Miss Pross, who takes Ladybird off R

Carton sits

Carton How quickly she is growing.

Everyone agrees

Mr Lorry enters L

Dr Manette (*standing*) Jarvis, my good fellow. Please sit down and enjoy a glass of wine.
Lorry Oh, I'm sorry. I hope I'm not interrupting anything.
Darnay My dear man, any such interruption by you is greeted with much pleasure. Please join us.
Lorry I must speak with you and Dr Manette.
Darnay But of course. (*He indicates to Lorry to sit at the table*)
Lorry Oh, it's only business matters and much too boring to spoil a lovely day like this. Perhaps we could talk in the garden?
Dr Manette We may speak by the lake.

Dr Manette, Darnay and Mr Lorry move L, watched by Lucie and Carton. The Lights cross fade to L

Lorry I didn't want to alarm your family, so I thought it would be better said in private.
Dr Manette So what's all the fuss about, my friend?

Lorry I received a letter at the bank addressed for Charles. (*He takes a letter from his pocket and hands it to Darnay*) I must apologize for opening it but I read all the mail that is sent to the bank. You must be aware of the threats that my colleagues and I receive.

Dr Manette Of course, Jarvis. But why the concern?

Lorry It is from an old servant of Charles's. He is imprisoned in La Forge. He is requesting Charles's help.

Dr Manette But how can Charles help?

Darnay (*finishing reading the letter*) I must go to France. I must save him.

Lorry But Charles, there is nothing you can do. France has fallen, danger lies around every corner.

Darnay The citizens will not harm me, I have denounced my family name and wealth.

Lorry What about your family here, in England?

Darnay I have no choice, I have to go. I gave this man my word, my sacred vow, that no harm should come to him whilst I lived.

Lorry Dr Manette, I beg you, talk some sense into his young mind.

Dr Manette Charles, you know how I feel about you ... I love you like a son, you are a part of my family, and I know I don't have to point out your responsibilities, especially now Lucie's with child again. But you must remember she's not strong and news of this could have an adverse effect on her. (*He pauses*) Will I be able to change your mind?

Darnay Sir, you have been much more than a blood father to me. I love you, just as I love your daughter and my own daughter. But you must understand that I made a vow that I cannot dishonour now.

Dr Manette Then I, my dear Charles, must respect your honour and wish you safe passage.

Lorry Dr Manette ——

Dr Manette I understand honour, Jarvis. In my past I, too, had to make such a decision.

Lorry Then, Charles, I shall travel with you.

Darnay There is no need, Mr Lorry.

Lorry I have bank business in France that I have neglected lately. We shall make the passage together.

Darnay opens his mouth to protest

(*Holding up his hands to stop Darnay's protest*) And no arguments.

Darnay (*to Dr Manette*) Please do not mention this to Lucie until after I have set sail.

Dr Manette As you wish, my son.

The Lights crossfade to R

Carton I must thank you for allowing me to join with your family.

Lucie We always enjoy your company, Sydney.

Carton And I yours, Lucie. (*He drinks his wine*)

Lucie Do you see me as a good friend, Sydney?

Carton Why, of course.

Lucie Then would you allow me, as a friend, to give you some advice?

Carton (*uncertainly*) Yes.

Lucie There's really no need to drink so much — it doesn't solve anything.

Carton (*laughing*) I take to *this* vice (*he holds up his glass*) better than
I ever did to *ad*vice, I'm afraid, Lucie. And besides, what better place
to hide?

Lucie But, surely, you *could* change your life?

Carton There was a time when I looked to you, this house, your family
and I thought that there was a different way for me. But now it's too late
to change. I shall never be better than I am. I am like one who has died
young.

Lucie If only you would let me help you.

Carton It's only you that does help me. (*He now becomes more intense
and speaks in an intimate tone*) But you can never return the love I have
for you; and all these vices you see before you now, I will yield to, time
and time again.

Lucie Can I? (*She pauses*) Can I not turn your affection for me towards
a better cause?

Carton All that you could do for me has been done. (*He pauses and takes
her hand in his*) But you must believe me when I say that I would
embrace any sacrifice for you. Indeed, I would gladly give my life for
you ... and your family.

Carton kisses Lucie's hand

Black-out

Music 25: You Must Go, My Friend

SCENE 3

Paris. The Guillotine

A guillotine has been set up c

A crowd of Peasants is on stage, lined up on either side of the guillotine; among them is Madame Defarge, who is knitting, as usual. A group of Soldiers stands R, guarding several Aristocrats

There is a drum roll. An Aristocrat is led to the guillotine. The Peasants crowd round to watch. The drum roll stops. The guillotine blade falls and the Peasants scream in delight. They all return to their original places and await the next victim. (The above routine is repeated each time an Aristocrat is beheaded)

First Peasant We have our revenge. France is the people's!
Second Peasant Look at how they fear us.
Madame Defarge Our revenge will not be complete until the last drop of aristocrat blood has dried.
Third Peasant Rejoice with our friend.

Music 26: Madame Guillotine

Peasants   She's the lady all the nobles die to meet.
                      I have seen a thousand heads fall at her feet.
                      Oh, she's a conversation killer,
                      Yes, she really is a scream,
                      That most delightful,
                      Rather frightful,
                      Madame Guillotine.

There is a drum roll. The execution routine begins again with the next Aristocrat

                      As they walk her wooden steps to paradise,
                      They will find her steel embrace as cold as ice,
                      Because although she isn't choosy
                      She prefers them soft and clean,

That most delightful,
Rather frightful,
Madame Guillotine.

Another drum roll. Another execution

Put on your best beret,
Don't let the wind blow it away,
There's a lady up there waiting
And it might just be your day.
Put on your best beret,
Don't let the wind blow it away,
There's a lady up there waiting
And it might just be your day.

Another drum roll. Another execution

Fetch a bottle and something that you can eat,
Fetch your woman and her knitting and a seat,
Then with the clicking of the needles,
Oh, perhaps they'll knit a web,
To encompass all the gentry
So that she can steal their heads.

She's the lady all the nobles die to meet.
I have seen a thousand heads fall at her feet.
Oh, she's a conversation killer,
Yes, she really is a scream,
That most delightful,
Rather frightful,
Madame Guillotine.

During the next verse, the Peasants exit, leaving Madame Defarge alone

Put on your best beret,
Don't let the wind blow it away,
There's a lady up there waiting
And it might just be your day.

Put on your best beret,
Don't let the wind blow it away,
There's a lady up there waiting
And it might just be your day.

Darnay is brought on by a group of Soldiers, R; *he is plainly under arrest. He is thrown on to the ground in front of Madame Defarge, who stands over him, menacingly*

Mme Defarge D'Evrémonde, allow me the pleasure to gloat. D'Evrémonde, Monsieur d'Evrémonde, how feared you look. (*She spits in in his face*) Go join your family. In Hell.

She exits R. *The Soldiers pick Darnay up and lead him off* R

The Lights fade to Black-out

Music 27: I Wonder What I'd Do (*Reprise*)

SCENE 4

England. Dr Manette's garden

Lucie enters L *reading a letter*

Music 28: I Wonder What I'd Do (*Reprise*)

Lucie   Whatever would I do
In a world that's without you?
Would it just become a place that's filled with pain?
Like a flower-scented breeze,
Lost among the lonely trees,
An empty soul left waiting for the rain.

And now there is nowhere else to hide
I'll come and stand right by your side,
And when the child beside me starts to cry
It's a part of us that can never die.

I wonder where I'd be,
I wonder where I'd be,
I wonder where I'd be
Without you.

She appears about to faint

Dr Manette enters L

Dr Manette Lucie, Lucie are you ailing?

Lucie I'm all right, Father, but it's Charles. He's been arrested and he's in La Forge. (*She pauses*) I must go to him.

Dr Manette No, I won't allow it. You're not fit to travel such a distance. We must consider your condition. I can't imagine what I would do, if you came to any harm. What would Charles think?

Lucie He needs me, Father, and I need him. I must go.

Dr Manette (*gently pulling Lucie to him, embracing her and patting her hair*) I understand, my child. Miss Pross and I will come too.

Lucie (*pulling away*) No!

Dr Manette The citizens will listen to me. They know me. Charles is my son. I must come with you   I will come with you.

Lucie Thank you.

They embrace again

The Lights fade to Black-out

Music 29: This Time For Us (*Reprise*)

SCENE 5

France. The Revolutionary Tribunal

A courtroom. The President (judge) is seated C with the Prosecutor beside him. The jury, L, is made up of ten Peasants, all wearing red berets. Dr Manette, Lucie and Ladybird, Miss Pross and Mr Lorry are sitting R, with Defarge and Madame Defarge (the latter knitting) standing behind them. The room is crowded with Peasants

A Seamstress is on the stand, being interrogated

Seamstress (*pleading*) I'm just a seamstress. I only worked for them.
Prosecutor Ah, but you *lived* with them.

The crowd reacts loudly to this

President (*shouting, but with an air of boredom*) I call for the verdict.

*Each Juror in a bored voice   this procedure has obviously become
routine — says "Guilty"*

I announce that the sentence for the enemy of the Republic is death,
death within twenty-four hours.

*The Peasants cheer The Seamstress is bundled towards the L exit by
Soldiers*

Darnay is brought on L by Soldiers

Call Charles d'Evrémonde.

The crowd jeers at Darnay

*The Seamstress stumbles and Darnay steadies her. He gives her a
reassuring smile*

The Seamstress is taken off

Carton enters and moves behind the Peasants

*No-one notices Carton except Miss Pross. She raises her hand in recog-
nition but Carton gestures to her to ignore him. Carton stands behind the
Peasants*

(*Ringing his bell; to Darnay*) You are accused under the decree which
forbids all aristocrats to return, under threat of death.
Darnay I was summoned to save an old servant of mine.

The crowd reacts to the word "servant"

Prosecutor Servant!
Darnay An old friend   a friend of the Republic!
Prosecutor The Public Prosecutor for this tribunal can announce that the
prisoner, Charles d'Evrémonde, called Darnay, has been denounced.

The crowd cheers

The prisoner has been denounced by three voices: Ernest Defarge, wine vendor, Thérèse Defarge, his wife, and Alexandre Manette, physician.

The crowd shouts again and is quietened by the President ringing his bell

Dr Manette (*jumping to his feet*) Monsieur le President, I protest to you, that this is a forgery and a fraud. Who and where is the false conspirator who says that I denounce the husband of my child?
Mme Defarge (*leaping forward and screaming*) I do!

The crowd reacts to this

Prosecutor I call upon Thérèse Defarge to speak to this tribunal.

Madame Defarge takes the stand

Mme Defarge (*removing Dr Manette's diary from her pocket*) Patriots, listen to me. I have in my hand a diary, in the writing of Dr Manette. He wrote this diary from the moment he was jailed. Sentenced because he tried to save the life of a dying woman, a woman who had been abused by Monsieur Philippe d'Evrémonde, uncle to the prisoner. The good doctor could not save this woman. She died from the injuries that d'Evrémonde inflicted upon her. (*She pauses*) And a part of me died that day also. Because that poor woman — (*she raises her voice*) — that poor woman was my sister.

The crowd reacts with horror

Yes, citizens, the d'Evrémondes murdered my family.

The crowd reacts noisily, screaming abuse at Darnay. They are finally silenced by the ringing of the President's bell

Listen to me. The words of Dr Manette. (*Reading from the diary*) "I now believe that the mark of the red cross is fatal to the house of d'Evrémonde, and that they have no part in God's mercies. I, Alexandre Manette, do, on this last night of the year seventeen seventy-six, in my unbearable agony, denounce them and their descendants, to the last of their race, and pray for the time when all these things shall be answered for. I denounce the d'Evrémondes to Heaven and to Hell ... (*screaming*) ... to Hell!

The crowd screams for Darnay's death. They are silenced by the President's bell

Save him now, my good doctor, save him now. (*She returns to her place and resumes her knitting*)

Again the crowd roars and has to be silenced by the President's bell

Dr Manette Monsieur le President, please ...
President I call for the verdict.

The jurors each say "Guilty" with great passion

President I announce that the sentence for the enemy of the Republic is death. Death within twenty-four hours.

The crowd screams with approval. Defarge and Madame Defarge stand together, talking

The President, the Prosecutor and the Peasants leave the courtroom

Soldiers move forward and start to lead Darnay away

Ladybird (*breaking away from Lucie and running towards Darnay*) Daddy!

Madame Defarge spins round and stares at Ladybird. Lucie rushes forward to comfort her child and is joined by Miss Pross

Darnay is led off

Miss Pross leads Lucie and her child off, Lucie looking back at Madame Defarge

Music 30: A Chance To Love

Defarge and Madame Defarge are DS, *Carton* US, *unseen by the others*

Defarge Why do you wait?

Mme Defarge I wish to savour this moment. It's been a great victory for us.

Defarge For you.

Mme Defarge For my family.

Defarge Will your conscience allow you to rest now? Has enough blood been spilled to satisfy your thirst?

Mme Defarge There are still two names left in my stitches.

Defarge It is complete, you have your revenge.

Mme Defarge Not yet, there are still two d'Evrémondes left.

Defarge No, no, you can't.

Mme Defarge My dear husband, how pitied you look. What happened to those words of freedom and justice you used to speak of?

Defarge We have won the justice; France is free now. Does that bitterness cloud your vision so, to blind you of this?

Mme Defarge Whilst that name still lives I have no freedom or justice.

Defarge For God's sake, woman. Can your heart be so shallow that you wish to kill a child?

Mme Defarge Did he question his heart whilst he was murdering my family?

Defarge They've done you no wrong.

Mme Defarge They carry the d'Evrémonde name.

Defarge It's just a name.

Mme Defarge Just a name. A name that carries the blood of my family on its hands.

Defarge You are destroying yourself. I cannot bear to witness this.

Mme Defarge And I cannot rest until my stitches are complete. And when they are, I can lay this shroud over my sister's grave.

Defarge I beg you, stop this now. We have suffered so much.

Mme Defarge What do you know of suffering?

Defarge turns away from Madame Defarge

(*Shouting at Defarge's back*) Monsieur Defarge, the Great Crusader, Liberator of all men. You win all yet lose nothing.

Defarge (*spinning round on her· screaming*) I'm losing my wife. (*Quieter*) Thérèse   I don't know you any more.

Defarge storms off R. *Madame Defarge exits* R *after a moment*

Carton, watching Madame Defarge go, comes DS

Miss Pross enters L

Miss Pross Sydney!

Carton heads towards her

Why are you here?

Carton To see if I can be of some assistance.

Miss Pross I wish you could, but we've tried everything.

Carton Maybe not. How about the doctor? Is there anyone else he could go to?

Miss Pross He has exhausted every possibility.

Carton And Mr Lorry? How about his business associates?

Miss Pross I am afraid that our last hope has gone.

Carton How is Lucie coping?

Miss Pross She's inconsolable.

Carton (*with his head bowed, deep in thought*) Maybe there is one last chance ...

Miss Pross What do you mean?

Carton I must secure you to a promise.

Miss Pross But of course.

Carton (*producing a document from his pocket*) This is a certificate that enables me to pass out of France. Sydney Carton, Englishman. Keep it for me until tomorrow.

Miss Pross But why?

Carton Because I would rather not have it in my possession when I visit Charles tomorrow in prison. Be sure that you have the certificates of the doctor, Lucie and the little one.

Miss Pross But surely you don't believe they're in danger also?

Carton (*holding both her arms to emphasize the danger*) Nobody connected with the d'Evrémonde house is safe now. (*He lets go of her*) Check your own certificate, as well as that of Mr Lorry.

Miss Pross looks worried

Don't look so dismayed, you have the opportunity to save them.

Miss Pross I? Oh, Heaven bless that I could. But how?

Carton Arrange for two carriages and horses for tomorrow. They must be ready by two o'clock in the afternoon. Tell Lucie and the doctor of the great danger for them in France and that they must leave at once. One of the carriages must be outside the house; Mr Lorry will organize the belongings. Have the second carriage waiting outside La Forge. The moment my place is occupied, drive away ——

Miss Pross But ——

Carton (*cutting her short*) — and then for England. Promise me solemnly that nothing will alter the course that we now stand pledged to one another.

Miss Pross (*with tears in her eyes*) Nothing will. (*She pauses, reaches out and touches him*) If I've misunderstood you before, Sydney, believe me, I regret it.

Carton You've never misunderstood me, Prossy, oh no. But had you wasted the whole of your life, having done no good at all, having secured no-one's love or affection or even regard and then one day you had a chance, just a small chance, to make some good of it all: could you then just waste that chance as well?

Miss Pross I don't know.

Carton Well, don't you see, with that one small sacrifice, perhaps all those young years would not have been wasted after all.

Miss Pross But your youth was never wasted.

Carton True, but my young way was never the way to age.

Carton exits L

After a short pause, Miss Pross exits R

Music 31: The Looking-Glass (*Reprise*)

Scene 6

France. Outside the cells of La Forge

A group of Soldiers is escorting Darnay across the stage, L *to* R

Lucie, Dr Manette and Miss Pross enter L, *see Darnay and follow him*

Lucie (*nearly crying*) Charles!
Darnay (*turning*) Lucie!

Darnay tries to break free of his escort. The Soldiers try to restrain him but then let him go. Lucie and Darnay embrace. Then Darnay catches sight of Dr Manette

Darnay Father ... sir ... I didn't know. My uncle ... (*He pauses*) Please forgive me. (*He breaks away from Lucie and holds his head in his hands*)
Dr Manette There is nothing to forgive. (*He grasps Darnay's shoulders and kisses him on both cheeks*)
Darnay Please take care of Lucie and ...
Dr Manette I will, my son, I will.

The Soldiers drag Darnay R

Darnay (*as he goes*) I love you, Lucie ...

The Soldiers and Darnay leave R

Lucie faints; Miss Pross and Dr Manette catch her

Carton enters L. He immediately goes to Lucie's aid

Dr Manette Mr Carton, I don't believe it. You're in France?
Carton Please, I will explain later. Now go to your carriage and I will bring Lucie.

Miss Pross leads Dr Manette off L, leaving Carton holding Lucie

Carton Remember my vow, my darling. (*He kisses Lucie's cheek*)

Music 32: The Looking-Glass (*Reprise*)

(*Singing*)
   I could easily allow myself to dream
   In the hope that sometimes
   Miracles come true,
   But my heart would never let my mind be free
   To forget the promise I once made to you.

I have walked along both paths of love and freedom
And found that freedom can be kind when love is cruel,
But it seems I never found a thing until I lost it
When the looking-glass is looking at a fool,
When the looking-glass is looking at a fool,
When the looking-glass is looking at a fool.

Carton carries Lucie off L

Music 33: Drums in La Forge

SCENE 7

France. In the cells of La Forge

There is a cell R, a corridor leads from the L to the cell door

Darnay is in the cell, sitting at a table, writing

Carton and Barsad enter L

Barsad (*stopping Carton, angrily*) How can I trust that you will not talk?
Carton Have you any choice? I do not believe that the citizens would
  rejoice in your past. Spying for the aristocrats? That would surely mean
  death.
Barsad What if something goes wrong? I'm telling you, there is no escape
  from La Forge.
Carton Just follow my instructions, my good fellow, and everything shall
  go according to plan.
Barsad (*realizing that he has no option*) Follow me.

  Barsad leads Carton R to Darnay's cell, then exits L

Darnay (*looking up from his writing, then standing, astonished*) Sydney,
  of all the people upon this Earth ——
Carton   you least expected to see me.
Darnay I do not believe it to be you. You're not a prisoner as well, are you?
Carton No, I come from Lucie. I bring a request from her.

Darnay What is it?

Carton You have no time to ask me why I bring it or what it means and I have no time to tell you. Just take off your jacket and put on mine.

Darnay Why?

Carton We have no time. Do as I say.

They swap their jackets during the following dialogue

Darnay Sydney, there is no escaping from this place, it can never be done. You will only die here. It is madness.

Carton Do I ask you to escape? If I ask you to pass out that door, tell me it is madness and remain here. Now, there is a pen on the table. Write what I dictate.

Darnay Why?

Carton Don't ask questions, just do it.

Darnay (*going to the table and preparing to write*) To whom do I address it?

Carton No-one. Now write these words. "If you remember the words that passed between us, long ago, you will readily comprehend this when you see it."

Carton takes a bottle of chloroform and a rag from his pocket during the following dialogue. He pours chloroform on to the rag and waits behind Darnay

Darnay What words? (*He looks up*)

Carton Keep writing ... "I am thankful that the time has come when I can prove them. That I do so is no subject for regret or grief."

Darnay finishes writing and raises his head. Carton grabs Darnay from behind and pushes the rag over his mouth. Darnay struggles and then passes out, his arms out in front of him

(*Writing on the page under Darnay's note*) "Dearest Lucie ... with much love, Sydney Carton." (*He folds up the paper and moves to put it into Darnay's pocket. He hesitates, then slips the paper up the sleeve of the jacket Darnay is wearing*

Music 34: You Must Go, My Friend

(Singing)   I brought a smile to her
But you're the one.
I brought a little light,
You brought the sun.
I would give anything
To be like you.
You'd be so right for her,
I'd be the fool.

Chorus   So you must go my friend
And I must stay.
Go to the one we love,
Take her away,
For you must live, my friend
And I must die
Don't let her know the reason why;
It's easier to lie.
Oh, please don't make her cry.

While others faced the world
I danced and sang,
Hiding behind the crowd
A lonely man,
But in my empty room
I saw the truth:
A pillow wet with tears
That held the proof.

Repeat chorus

The words I could not find
Will lie in peace within my mind.
The things I feel today
Are all the things I never
Had the chance to say.

Repeat the first verse

Chorus   So you must go, my friend
                          And I must stay.
                          Go to the one we love,
                          Take her away,
                          For you must live, my friend
                          And I must die
                          Don't let her know the reason why;
                          It's easier to lie.
                          Please give her my goodbye.

(*Speaking*) Guard! Guard! (*He turns his back to the door*)

Barsad and the Soldiers run on L

(*Speaking*) Don't be alarmed. Mr Carton is somewhat overcome. Please
escort him to his carriage.

*The Soldiers look to Barsad enquiringly. He gestures to them to pick
Darnay up. As they lift him, Carton looks intently at Barsad. Barsad
returns his gaze*

Barsad, the Soldiers and Darnay leave L

Music 35: You Must Go, My Friend (*Reprise*)

(*Singing*)   I brought a smile to her
                          But you're the one.
                          I brought a little light,
                          You brought the sun.
                          I would give anything
                          To be like you.
                          You'd be so right for her,
                          I'd be the fool.

Chorus   So you must go my friend.
                          Go to the one we love,
                          Take her away,
                          For you must live, my friend
                          And I must die

Don't let her know the reason why;
It's easier to lie.
Just give her my goodbye.

Black-out

Music 36: Madame Guillotine (*Reprise*)

SCENE 8

France. Outside Dr Manette's house

Madame Defarge stands c, *holding a loaded pistol*

Several Peasants enter R

First Peasant Thérèse, why are you waiting here? It is the day we kill the D'Evrémonde name.
Mme Defarge There are still two d'Evrémondes left. The wife and child. I wait for them.
First Peasant (*excitedly*) Why don't we go in and bring them out? I'll go and get your husband and ——
Mme Defarge (*shouting*) No! (*Then quieter*) I must do this for myself. I cannot trust my husband now. He does not understand. Take this ... (*she hands her knitting to the First Peasant*) ... and put this at my usual place by the guillotine. I'll be there soon to see d'Evrémonde's head. My shroud is soon to be complete.

The First Peasant laughs and exits R; *the other Peasants follow*

Music 37: A Chance To Love

Mme Defarge   It's nearly through,
The final payment, so long overdue
Will now be paid in full.
I'm glad to be the tool,
Don't look to find a trace of sympathy in me.

A chance to love
Will come when time has healed this tortured land.

The hate we cannot hide
Will gradually subside,
And then perhaps we'll find
A chance to love.

No more talk about what could have been,
I will see it all reborn.
I tell you,
Love lies sleeping in my memory
Waiting for a friendly dawn.

Miss Pross, Lucie and Ladybird enter L, *dressed for travel*

Seeing Madame Defarge, Miss Pross pushes Lucie and Ladybird behind her, protectively. She approaches Madame Defarge

A chance to love
The man that stood beside me in the storm.
I hope he'll try to see
Some tenderness in me,
And then at last
We'll have a chance to love.

Madame Defarge turns, brandishing her pistol. She advances menacingly on Miss Pross and her party

Miss Pross   A chance to love,
To give them time to find a chance to love
I'll face the hate in you
And do what I must do.
No-one should be denied a chance to love.

Miss Pross ⎫ It's nearly through,
Mme Defarge ⎭ The final payment, so long overdue
Will now be paid in full.
I'm glad to be the tool,
No-one should be denied a chance to love.

Miss Pross and Madame Defarge fight hand-to-hand, the pistol being held between them at waist height. The pistol fires. Madame Defarge clutches her stomach and stands motionless. Miss Pross staggers back, horrified

Defarge enters R, *at a run*

Defarge Thérèse!

Madame Defarge turns to him, stretching out a hand for support. He rushes forward as she begins to fall, and catches her Her beret falls off. She dies in his arms

(*To Miss Pross*) Go!

Miss Pross stands stunned

Go!

Miss Pross, Lucie and Ladybird run off L

(*Singing*)   How long it's been
Since I have seen you sleep so peacefully.
I see again in you
The girl that I once knew
Before we both got taken by the tide.

All of our dreams
Are empty now, I'm left here on my own
And every dawn I find
Will just serve to remind
Me of the time, we wasted without love.

Instrumental interlude. Defarge caresses Madame Defarge's face and picks up her fallen beret

A chance to love,
We won it all yet lost the chance to love.
You'll never get to see the tenderness in me
We'll never have, have the chance to love,
Have the chance to love,
Have the chance to love.

Black-out

Music 38: A Chance To Love (*Reprise*)

SCENE 9

France. The guillotine

The guillotine has been set up as in Act II Scene 3

Soldiers and Peasants are waiting for the executions to begin

Two Aristocrats, Carton and the Seamstress are brought in by soldiers

Second Peasant Where is Thérèse Defarge?
First Peasant She must come. I've got her knitting here and there's an
   empty space for her.

*There are three drum taps, during which the first Aristocrat is led to the
guillotine. As the Aristocrat reaches the guillotine there is a drumroll. The
Peasants crowd round to watch. The drum roll stops. The guillotine blade
falls and the Peasants scream with delight. They return to their original
places. The sequence begins again, with the second Aristocrat. The
following dialogue takes place as the Aristocrat is led to the guillotine*

Seamstress (*to Carton*) Please sir, I am just a seamstress. I have done no
   wrong. Why do they wish to kill me?
Carton Fear, my dear child. They act from fear.
Seamstress But I'm afraid. I'm so afraid of death.
Carton Hold my hand.

*The Seamstress takes Carton's hand as the drum roll sounds. The
guillotine blade falls and the peasants cheer As they disperse, the
Seamstress tries to see the decapitated body beyond the guillotine*

(*Taking the Seamstress's face in his hands and turning it to face him*) Keep
   your eyes on me, my child, and mind no other object.
Seamstress (*taking both his hands in hers*) I mind nothing while I hold
   your hand.

They lower their hands, still holding on to each other

   I shall mind nothing when I let it go, if they are rapid.
Carton They will be rapid; don't be afraid.

A Guard approaches them

Guard Out of the way, d'Evrémonde. We're saving you 'til last.

The Guard shoves Carton in the queue behind the Seamstress and returns to his original place

Seamstress (*studying Carton's face, then pointing at him*) But you're not —

Carton covers her pointing finger with his hand and shakes his head to silence her

  Why?
Carton He was my friend.
Seamstress But you're going to die.
Carton (*calmly*) Yes.
Seamstress You almost seem to welcome it.
Carton Maybe in death I can secure a place in the hearts of the ones I love.
Seamstress You're a brave and good man.

The drum taps begin again. Carton looks over towards the guillotine

Seamstress (*staring at Carton*) Is it my turn? Has the moment come?
Carton (*facing her*) Yes, we must say goodbye, now. (*He kisses her*)

Before the kiss is completed, the Soldiers drag the Seamstress away to the guillotine. The execution is carried out. As the guillotine blade comes down, Carton winces. The crowd parts as before. A drumroll begins. The Soldiers lead Carton to the guillotine

  (*Turning to the audience*) It is a far, far better thing I do than I have ever done. It is a far, far better rest I go to than I have ever known.

The crowd gathers round as before

Black-out

CURTAIN

The CURTAIN *is down*

The eerie sounds as heard at the beginning of the play, are heard again, they continue under the following voice-over

Voice   Enter any great city
                     When every soul is asleep
                     Can you imagine all the secrets they must keep?
                     It's an odd fascination
                     But when you look it's so true
                     That the strangest of strangers
                     Is no stranger, stranger than you.

The CURTAIN *rises*

The stage is completely bare

The Soloist is alone, C. *She begins the following song and is joined, as it progresses, by the rest of the cast, principals first, singing and taking up positions around the stage*

Music 39: A Tale of Two Cities

Soloist   It's just a tale of two cities
                     Maybe yours or maybe mine;
                     A tale of the people
                     From some other time.
                     A lady loved, loved by two
                     And how others could feel;
                     An ageing shoemaker
                     Locked in the Bastille.

All (*Chorus*)   Enter any great city
                     When every soul is asleep.
                     Can you imagine all the secrets they must keep?
                     Well, the strangest of strangers,
                     When you look it's so true,
                     Is no stranger, stranger than you.

It's just a tale of foolishness
That caused misery and grief,
Leaving words of wisdom
In a sea of disbelief.
It was a dream filled with promise
That came to the light
Only to discover
It was shattered in the fight.

Repeat chorus

It's just a tale of two lovers
In the cold hands of fate,
Amid the French Revolution,
Amid the blindness of hate,
Of the poor Sydney Carton
And noble Darnay.
It's a tale for all lovers
In some other day.

Repeat chorus

It's just a tale of a drunkard
Who gave his love and his life,
As he walked for the lovers
To the guillotine knife.
It's a far, far better thing I do
Than I have ever done before;
To a far, far better rest I go,
Than I have ever known for sure.

Repeat chorus

Well, the strangest of strangers,
But when you look it's so true.
Is no stranger, stranger than you.

CURTAIN

FURNITURE AND PROPERTY LIST

ACT I

Tables
Stools
Chairs
Market stalls *On them*: goods for sale
Defarge's crates of wine bottles
Gaspard's grey beret
Madame Defarge's knitting
Coins
Wine glasses
Bottles
Dr Manette's workbench *On it*: shoemaking equipment
Defarge: Dr Manette's diary
Legal documents
Stryver's coat
Jerry Cruncher's note
Gaspard's knife
Garden bench
Miss Pross's skein of wool
Lucie's fan
Soldiers' rifles
Peasants' weapons
Wine goblets
Madame Defarge's pistol

ACT II

Defarge's flag
Peasant's weapons
Garden table
Garden chairs
Wine bottles
Glasses
Lorry's letter
Soldiers' rifles
Lucie's letter
Bell
Madame Defarge; Dr Manette's diary
Carton's document
Table
Chair
Writing paper
Pen
Inkwell
Carton's bottle of chloroform
Rag
Madame Defarge's pistol
Madame Defarge's knitting

LIGHTING PLOT

ACT I: Prologue

To open   Darkness

Cue 1   When ready   (Page 1)
           Bring up spot on **Soloist**

ACT I, Scene 1

To open.   General exterior lighting

No cues

ACT I, Scene 2

To open: Exterior lighting ʀ only

No cues

ACT 1, Scene 3

To open.   Interior lighting on wine shop set only

Cue 2   **Defarge** leads **Lucie** to the workshop   (Page 9)
           Cross-fade from wine shop to workshop

Cue 3   **Lucie** and **Dr Manette** enter the wine shop   (Page 10)
           Cross-fade from workshop to wine shop

Cue 4   **Madame Defarge**: "... fight for our freedom."   (Page 12)
           Fade lights to black-out

ACT I, Scene 4

To open.   General interior lighting

No cues

ACT I, Scene 5

To open. General interior lighting

Cue 5   **Barsad: "... definitely British and secret."**   (Page 14)
             Slowly fade lights on main courtroom area; lights
             remain on L

Cue 6   **Jerry Cruncher** exits   (Page 15)
             Bring lights up on courtroom

ACT I, Scene 6

To open: General interior lighting

Cue 7   **Madame Defarge: "I have many things to plan."** (Page 20)
             Fade lights on set, bring up spots L *and* R

Cue 8   End of Music 13   (Page 21)
             Black-out

ACT I, Scene 7

To open. General interior lighting

No cues

ACT I, Scene 8

To open. General interior lighting

Cue 9   **Gaspard** hides on the balcony   (Page 28)
             Spot up on **Gaspard,** *lights down on rest of*
             ballroom

Cue 10   **Gaspard: "... sort of second cousins to the King."** (Page 28)
             Fade spot, bring lights up on ballroom

ACT I, Scene 9

To open. General exterior lighting

Cue 11   **Darnay and Lucie** cross from c to l   (Page 30)
            Cross-fade lights from c *to* l

Cue 12   **Darnay and Lucie** return   (Page 30)
            Cross-fade lights from l *to* c

Cue 13   **Darnay** takes **Dr Manette** r   (Page 31)
            Cross-fade lights from c *to* r

Cue 14   **Darnay:** "My name was Charles D'Evrémonde." (Page 32)
            Lights fade; spot up on **Carton**, l

Cue 15   **Carton** (*singing*): "The way that I am."   (Page 32)
            Spot up on **Darnay** *and* **Lucie** r

Cue 16   End of Music 20   (Page 32)
            Black-out

ACT 1, Scene 10

To open. General exterior lighting

No cues

ACT II, Scene 1

To open. General exterior lighting

No cues

ACT II, Scene 2

To open. General exterior lighting

Cue 17	**Dr Manette:** "We may speak by the lake." *Cross-fade lights from* R *to* L	(Page 39)
Cue 18	**Dr Manette:** "As you wish, my son." *Cross-fade lights to* R	(Page 41)
Cue 19	**Carton** kisses **Lucie's** hand *Black-out*	(Page 41)

ACT II, SCENE 3

To open. General exterior lighting

Cue 20	**Soldiers** lead **Darnay** off R *Fade to Black-out*	(Page 44)

ACT II, SCENE 4

To open: General exterior lighting

Cue 21	**Lucie** and **Dr Manette** embrace *Fade to Black-out*	(Page 45)

ACT II, SCENE 5

To open: General exterior lighting

No cues

ACT II, SCENE 6

To open. General exterior lighting

No cues

ACT II, SCENE 7

To open: General interior lighting

Cue 22	End of Music 35 *Black-out*	(Page 57)

70

ACT II, SCENE 8

To open.   General exterior lighting

Cue 23   End of Music 37   (Page 59)
            Black-out

ACT II, SCENE 9

To open.   General exterior lighting

Cue 24   The crowd gathers round **Carton**   (Page 61)
            Black-out

EPILOGUE

To open: Darkness

Cue 25   The CURTAIN rises   (Page 61)
            Bring up general lighting

EFFECTS PLOT

Cue 1   **Gaspard** returns to the table   (Page 3)
           Carriage approaches

Cue 2   **First Child** runs off R; after a moment   (Page 3)
           Thud as carriage hits Child